THE PSYCHOLOGY OF PERSUASION

THE PSYCHOLOGY OF PERSUASION

SLOANE MONTGOMERY

CONTENTS

CHAPTER 1

Introduction to Persuasion and Influence

Two questions have persisted throughout human history: "What makes people change another person's mind?" (How are people persuaded?) and "Why do individuals decide to change their minds or alter their behavior?" (How do people make decisions?) These questions process psychological processes, from basic perception to the development of complex reasoning and intelligence.

Persuasion is an active form of social influence that seeks to change beliefs, feelings, or behaviors. Persuasion typically involves attempting to change the beliefs, feelings, or behaviors of another person one-on-one, as opposed to mass audience persuasion, which occurs during person-to-mass media interactions, such as in large social movements and political propaganda. Influence is a broader term that refers to how people affect our thoughts, feelings, and behaviors within a social context. Influence includes compliance, conformity, obedience, leadership, and group processes. Topics such as prejudice, aggression, and close relationships can all be considered under the influence umbrella because they are ways we affect and are affected by others. In this chapter, we focus on traditional persuasion. It is a powerful activity; it can free prisoners from jails while making free people feel like prisoners.

Definition and Importance of Persuasion

Nonverbal persuasion can be an effective and influential force. Persuasion can be employed to influence a number of outcomes. Persuasion is a staple of polemical and many other types of writing as well as advertising, political speeches, commercials, and letters to the editor. Group members persuade through public debate and often must persuade in order to continue in organizational conduct. Our practices, then, are rife with persuasion. Individuals attempt to influence the actions and attitudes of others in everyday conversation. Successful employment of influence techniques requires a facility with the tools of persuasion. About 45 of every 60 minutes each day are spent communing. Few skills are more important.

Persuasion can be viewed as an amalgam of science and art. Knowledge about and appropriate use of persuasion is beneficial in many avenues of life. Persuasion is the process by which a message induces change in beliefs, attitudes, or behaviors. It is closely related to the concept of influence, which refers to change across a wide range of topics. Unlike demagogues who tend toward hidden or distorted purposes, persuaders attempt to use openness to make convincing claims. Most information is engaged and created with an intent to influence. Persons can process subliminal messages that can prime individual activity automatically, barring dissimilar attitudes.

Historical Perspectives on Influence

In the Middle Ages, philosophers and theologians like Thomas Aquinas attempted to define and explain willpower, freedom, and rule following and began to consider their implications for morality and moral actions. As the philosophical questions about influence were being raised and explained, concepts relating to human nature, personality, motivation, groups, and the like were the province of the philosophical and humanistic classical tradition. These early ideas formed the basis for the more scholarly study of influence relationships. By the nineteenth century, modern empirical social psychology began. Scientists interested in the psychology of decision-making and response selection first began to develop and test various hypotheses about influence and persuasion. However, even these early attempts at research and theorizing about these matters owed much to the earlier philosophical arguments and commonplace observations found in the literary record.

When psychologists and researchers first began to study influence and persuasion, they borrowed heavily from disciplines such as philosophy, sociology, communications, and marketing. References can be found in literature dating prior to 2500 BC alluding to the fact that people have always been aware of instances of influence and persuasion. The beginnings of ideas in the Western tradition are easier to identify and can be traced back to the writings of the ancient Greeks. For example, Socrates and Plato discussed how the spoken word had the power to move or affect people. Aristotle wrote about rhetorical persuasion, which he said was the art of finding in any given case the available means of persuasion. The ancient Greek poets also wrote about how persuasion led men to act against their interests, using tricks and passion to manipulate them.

CHAPTER 2

Cognitive Processes in Decision-Making

A conspicuous feature of the history of the study of information processes is how often it has been rediscovered. The scholars in psychology and this in the ancient world appeared to have rediscovered, reinvented, or reformulated it in virtually every century from the time of the Greeks until the present era. The most recent formulations emerge in a culture still primarily distinguished by empirical methods of studying human beings. The basic models are, quite consistently, straightforwardly intellectual - we see human beings, in essence as "thinking machines".

Central to any model of how decision-making is influenced by persuasive messages are the cognitive processes to which such messages are directed. Any message must pass through these processes eventually to be related to the content of prior knowledge if it is to exert any influence on subsequent behavior. Although it is beyond the aims of an essay such as the present one to give a full account of the current state of knowledge of the process of information processing, the urgency to develop such models does alert us to the gaps in current knowledge.

Dual Process Theory

The dual system has cores and peripheries that change through development and intervention. More stable personality differences have a biological basis, including genetics and speed of information processing. Moods and anxieties affect which automatic or controlled processes operate. Social and interpersonal cues, like non-verbal behaviors, can trigger particular automatic or controlled responses, as can certain words or incentives. The controlled-automatic system has multiple semantic and emotional links to similar words, meaning prime words can affect how control is exerted over operations. Suggestions may bias our perceptions or inhibit our current desires. In times of need or particular usefulness, the prime will become dominant. The prime only gets inhibited if we notice we're at risk.

Fiske and Taylor introduced several concepts used to describe the dual system. They called the first system controlled processing. The second system controls automatic processing. According to Fiske and Taylor, controlled processing occurs while we think logically or rationally about problems. We use controlled processing if we need to solve complicated tasks or deal with uncertainty. Automatic processing is simple and effortless. It occurs behind our awareness, regardless of our intent or desire. Controlled processing has error rates, response latencies, and capacity limits. Automatic processing does not. Controlled processing takes place in sequence, meaning we attend to task demands one after another. Automatic processing occurs in parallel with no limit to how many automatic systems exist within one person, or how many levels of ideas or goals are primed at one time.

Heuristics and Biases

Decision-making models have the virtue of reducing a complex multicued probabilistic judgment task to one computed along a single dimension, but the models give rise to troubling error patterns. For example, since models depend on the weights provided to each cue, the researchers proposed the term weight degradation to account for the substantial breakdown in judgment quality when judges computed numeric scores for decision models.

The simple rules that people use to make decisions in their day to day lives may work fairly well in many areas, including shopping and arranging travel plans, but they leave considerable room for error in others, such as making choices in conditions of uncertainty or when stakes are high. In fact, these rules are particularly worrisome when they concern issues of safety and similar circumstances when wagers that are large or irreversible are involved. One aspect of this "decision-making by rules" is known as the use of heuristics—cognitive shortcuts that can help people save time and effort in making decisions. Heuristics enable a person to "discover facts" and make judgments, yet they give only approximations based on experiential decision making. To attribute these potential shortfalls in rational decision making only to heuristics, however, would certainly miss many individuals' decisions that were actually confirmatory and reinforce existing perceptual biases and stereotypes.

CHAPTER 3

Emotional and Motivational Factors in Persuasion

The message itself can elicit emotional and motivational responses from the recipient, thus allowing for psychological adjustment. It is worthwhile considering how the emotional and motivational nature of the recipients can be influenced. What urgency, personal identification, and emotional arousal are carried by the message as it is received? Can the message be further enhanced by its surroundings? Such questions thrust the analysis into the realm of empathy, an area in which the ability to reach desired goals depends heavily on the goal through examination of the person's entire profile: demographic factors, personality, interests, attitudes, and physiological and cognitive responses. Social roles and group influences also affect which attitudes are assumed and maintained, and how concerns of persuasive importance are channeled and may last over extended periods of time by different agents. Additionally, conditions that must be fulfilled.

Information and persuasion can be beneficial to the recipient by assisting them in forming judgments, making choices, and setting goals. Given our enormous need for these functions, it is not surprising that to be even a passive agent in the persuasive process can be extremely costly. How often do people have something to gain from having their tastes and beliefs manipulated? When we are uncertain or when our ego is assuaged by misleading others about our abilities, the passive acquisition of persuasion may be advantageous. Why do we let ourselves be persuaded? The theories and concepts examined in this book help us determine the emotional and motivational reasons behind people's propensity to change attitudes and believe that others control their ability to learn.

What leads us to adopt certain attitudes or make specific choices? Although we often attribute our decisions to rational considerations, laboratory experiments demonstrate that often this is not the case. In everyday life, innumerable internal and external mechanisms are influencing how we perceive and interpret events. For this reason, persuasion, although passive, can be more effective if it is able to manipulate the emotional and motivational dimensions that underlie attitudes, choices, and behavior.

Fear Appeals and Persuasion

In general, fear appeals may work to change attitudes by motivating people to think more deeply about the persuasive message. They also draw attention, being highly stimulating cognitive processes, and demonstrate the threat value to the individual. Research in health psychology has tested the effectiveness of various types of fear appeals, and a consistent pattern is that they are more persuasive when moderate amounts of fear are evoked compared to messages in which little fear or too much fear is evoked. Even people with strong predispositions, such as low self-esteem or belief in the invulnerability heuristic, may also be influenced by moderate fear appeals. Would-be persuaders who want to use fear appeals can often avoid evoking too much fear by providing recommendations about what to do, and how to avert the negative consequences of failing to comply with the message. However, because evoking moderate amounts of fear is difficult, and it is easy to evoke no fear, fear appeals are less commonly used than other appeal types used. A meta-analysis of the effectiveness of fear appeals in advertising found that fear appeals are no more persuasive than positive appeals. Besides, people often experience negative emotions when confronted by fear appeals, and this negative affect can result in reactance, or decreased intentions to comply with the recommended behavior. Combinations of fear appeals and other types of persuasive messages have surprisingly increased compliance with the message.

A fear appeal is a persuasive message that attempts to change people's attitudes by arousing their fears. The appeal outlines specific recommendations for avoiding harm and may present information about the probability and severity of harm related to the issue. Guilt appeals, which are less common and have been less widely researched, are messages that make people feel guilty if they do not comply.

Motivation and Persuasion

Persuaders potentially face an additional problem: some of the people who are unmotivated to think about an issue also have a firm opinion - one which is resistant to change. For people with strong attitudes, the processing of any additional corroborative information they might encounter is said to be biased in favor of the initial position. This phenomenon is known as the 'perceiver involvement effect' (or the 'pillow' hypothesis) and stems from the observation that, by providing extra information that supports the initial opinion, people can effectively 'pad' the supportive evidence for the opinion they have come to hold.

Decades of research have indicated the conditions when people are motivated to go in search of new information. For example, one key determinant seems to be the level of uncertainty they experience about the issue at hand. When people are certain, or feel certain, that they hold the right opinion, incurring the effort of searching through additional information to support that opinion is seen as an unnecessary cost. This leads to one important theoretical prediction: if an audience has a low level of uncertainty about an issue being discussed, the audience will remain relatively unmotivated to process the evidence being used for persuasion. When social psychologists talk about motivating an audience, they are usually referring to reducing uncertainty in the minds of an audience.

As mentioned at the start of the previous chapter, motivation is a critical determinant of a persuader's success - if people are motivated to arrive at an accurate judgment, they will not be readily influenced. However, what exactly do we mean by motivation - and under what circumstances are people motivated to go one way or the other?

CHAPTER 4

The Role of Communication in Persuasion

Ways of enhancing the persuasive effectiveness of any communication—spoken, written or any other medium—are therefore of immense interest. Not only is the technique of great interest to the direct persuader trying to change the viewpoint of another person, but to any communicator who seeks to change or reinforce attitudes through their work (i.e. politicians, leaders of organizations and rule making bodies) or who is required to develop a means of themselves resisting persuasion (i.e. defence lawyers and those doing interrogations or public interviews).

Communication is vitally important in the process of influence. Until you can develop a means of accurately sharing and promoting the ideas in your head with others, influencing is indeed a futile act. Nuts and bolts, however, are no guarantee of a quality building. Communication goes right to the heart of persuasion. Whilst it is possible to mechanically explain what needs to be proved (the central arguments), and the role of any additional material (peripheral arguments) that should be included, the actual ways in which the influencing targets these arguments are expressed is qualitative in nature.

Verbal and Nonverbal Communication

Nonverbal communication is so much more reliable than verbal communication. Yet, during the interview, only 8% of candidates are not hired because too many of their nonverbal etiquette errors are overwhelming. In order to manipulate someone, every minute, most people make approximately 157 nonverbal signals. People you meet expect you to behave like everyone else because your success as a communicator is affected by your "appropriateness." For interview judgment sufferers, law enforcement agents who have had no specialized training more readily detect deception when nonverbal signals are available. For people who distribute canned speeches, personal presentations rate more high credibility. In fact, personal presence predicts the best presenter. Networking skills, however, determine what a person gets paid and if a person is employed in most fields. Your nonverbal communication is critical, yet few realize how important it is to their professional success.

Most of our face-to-face communication is not spoken, yet most of our attention during business communication is verbal, especially the use of words, tone, medium, and transmitting of the message. In a year, the average human being utters enough words to fill 132 novels, smiles enough to fill 2,000 pages, shakes hands for up to eight hours, and spends 28% of the day communicating. For a successful business relationship, nonverbal cues are powerful ingredients; they can be used to influence, negotiate, delegate or project power and charisma. The result of a disappointing first impression is that 90% is based on nonverbal signals; 55% of communication is through body language, 38% through tone and seven through verbal content.

Message Framing

An example of how framing works is when information related to traffic accident injuries is presented using two different frames. One frame is the positive frame, which states that seat belts can save your life. The other frame is the negative frame, which states that if you forget to fasten the seat belts, even an accident at a speed of 15 mph could result in serious injury or death. In a study, it was found that in a situation with the positive frame, people are more likely to pay attention to the positive inner factors, such as life-saving aspects, when making a decision. And in a situation using the negative frame, people are more likely to pay attention to risk warning factors when making a judgment. The study shows that when the subjects were persuaded with the negative frame, they thought that the injuries in the accident were caused by their not wearing a seat belt, while the subjects who were persuaded using the positive frame thought that the injuries were caused by other factors, so wearing a seat belt did not assist them.

One of the key elements in messaging is framing. A frame is defined as the central organizing idea or focal point that puts the information in context. In communication, framing also means the power of selection in defining points of focus. Information collected under a certain frame means that other information collected under another frame will be blocked out. Information transmitted through a certain frame means that other information transmitted through another frame will also be blocked out. Under the same data, different frames yield different results. Linguistically, expressions like perspective, general understanding, and paradigm can be used as synonyms for frames.

CHAPTER 5

Social Influence and Conformity

In the face of these playful yet disquieting studies, a good many postgraduate students placed themselves in an unnecessary bind by refusing to turn the shock machine's dial to "off" when given the opportunity. The students felt they had no alternative other than to go forward to the fifteen switches nearest them, depressing first a predesignated one and then one or more unspecified switches up to the fifteenth, which did fire the tenth loud blast of surprise from the theorist. Their self-doubt is directly related to the recoil we feel when we defy the judgment of others. Everyone else was remaining in their seats, seemingly confident that they had made their considered choice and had concluded that not only were the demands of the experiment and the external legitimacy of the experimenter pulling them forward but that their own moral values were as well and there was no reason to hesitate. They were picturing themselves as decent, reasoning persons who, while they may have begun to feel guilty, never reached the stage of self-doubt that comes when we face a choice between what is right for us versus what brings us back into the good graces of others.

Normative Social Influence

A very similar type of behavior can be observed regarding the expression of group identification. The "seeking of evidence concerning personal identity by association to a relevant group" in order to reduce uncertainty about oneself and to control others' perceptions is a well-established concept in social psychology. A study by Bickers and Grotz illustrates this behavior well. In this experiment, if 33% of participants positively answer the question "Who am I?" with "Jaguar," 33% respond "Jaguar" in the subsequent question about which car manufacturer to use as the "Best friend" in the pseudo-social task.

Experiments have long shown that consistent majorities can change other people's private opinions, even when the subjects who change their views are certain that their initial opinion was correct. People tend to go along when they think their opinion is the unpopular one. This phenomenon of contorting oneself in order to fit in with the group has mainly been tested with regard to changing one's private opinion. While going along with the crowd in order to privately agree need not necessarily lead to public conformity as well, Kallgren, Cialdini, & Reno argue that "the person who dared not give the right answer in private is the same person who dares not express the right belief in public.

Informational Social Influence

Three factors contribute to the strength of informational social influence: 1. When the situation is ambiguous – when people are uncertain about what behaviors or actions are deemed appropriate, especially in unusual and novel situations, they are more likely to follow others. 2. When judgments are made in public – when people make decisions in a group such that others' reactions are public knowledge and must be faced, conformity is more likely to occur. 3.

When the event has important consequences – when a decision is seen as critical or has important consequences, there is a higher level of reliance on public opinion which produces a greater likelihood of conformity.

Informational social influence occurs when individuals derive conclusions about the truth of events based on the actions of others. Generally, when confronted with a novel or difficult task, individuals are likely to look to others to understand how they ought to behave. For example, people tend to buy more units of a product when they see other people buying the same thing because they believe the other people possess information they do not. This type of social influence is stronger when others are seen as similar and when individuals judge the task to be ambiguous.

CHAPTER 6

Ethical Considerations in Persuasion

Advertisers also have an increased ability to influence their current and potential customers through the use of social media and search engine advertisements. In an era of advertising personalization, advertisers have an important decision to make about whether or not to serve or block ads based on user behavior. Finally, individuals are placed under additional scrutiny. Ethical guidelines also apply to this group, which is often involved in objectionable practices such as pimping users for likes, shares, and appearances, profiles that advertise themselves on social media or through blog content by offering commercial incentives.

Not all persuasion intentions are unethical. However, even when persuasion scenarios are approached with good intentions, ethical concerns still need to be raised. Budd, Craig-Lees, and Mangan from the University of New England in Armidale, Australia suggested several ethical considerations illustrated in their article "From Opinion Leaders to Candidate Suggesters: Ethical Considerations of Persuasion in Social Networks?" In a digital communications environment, the potential for unethical behavior is heightened, due largely to the lack of oversight and barriers to entry. It is now easier than ever for organizations to spread unethical messages to their target audience. Furthermore, persuasive content in social media demands careful self-consideration. These government tactics may include finding and creating social media content and manipulating the behavior of online commentators.

Deception and Manipulation

These manipulative tactics attest to the fact that all is fair in love, war, and persuasion. While we generally consider persuasion to be a force of good, some of the other players in the great game of persuasion are better at deceiving and manipulating than others. Amnesty International uses persuasion to expose human rights abuses. No one, however, regards those who commit the abuses as good people persuading for the right reasons. Instead, we perceive their argument as manipulative and deceptive. As covert tactics, deception and manipulation indirectly undermine persuasive efforts. Only when an audience becomes aware of the ruse and realizes the true nature of the message does persuasion become bootless.

On the dark side of persuasion, manipulation can take the form of deception. We sometimes use persuasion to mislead others. We even shun out help, an act so unnatural it feels like the right thing to do. To deceive others, we frequently employ cues that experts in deception, especially criminal investigators, believe signal deceit. Lies are often told last minute, so keep a lookout for such verbal clues. In summary, a sharp jump in vocal quality often suggests lying. Nonverbal cues are also dropped when we are not telling the truth. Those who lie are less likely to make eye contact, and they touch their face or scratch their nose more often than those who tell the truth.

Informed Consent

Comprehension is essential for truly informed consent. However, most informed consent is given with a non-interactive written consent form. Readers may rush through the form without asking the questions that would indicate their true level of understanding. Even when a form is meticulously scrutinized, several factors can impede overall comprehension: literacy levels, emotional states, personal biases, the people challenging individuals to ask questions, linguistic differences and cultural negotiations of power and autonomy. Indeed, even our best educated college students and pioneers appear to have poor understanding when presented with traditional informed consent materials. Fewer than half of a representative sample of pioneers who participated in a standardized informed consent procedure remembered a majority of the information one day after the consent meetings.

Generally, research participants must give informed consent prior to their participation. Their decision should be based on an accurate portrayal of the study and the potential risks, including a discussion of the researchers' proposed solutions for the risks involved. In one study, women were more likely to volunteer for cervical cancer screening in a letter condition than in a letter-plus-pamphlet condition. The pamphlet presented worst-case scenarios regarding the disease and described the screening procedure. By emphasizing the potential risks, including bad news, the more comprehensive message caused the women to "feel less well-informed about the benefits and drawbacks of screening and they wanted a wider range of additional information".

CHAPTER 7

Strategies for Effective Persuasion

Credibility in persuasion refers to the communicator's trustworthiness and expertise. The perception of persuasiveness can be affected by the communicator's reputation, his mannerisms, and things such as prior position papers. Such factors create a general aura of believability around the speaker that is independent of the particular qualities of the speech. The upshot is that if someone is considered to be a sound and well-informed person, the listener is more likely to believe what is said. The listener will accept the conclusion to some extent based on the acceptance of the source.

Having examined the primary elements that make up the persuasion process, we now turn to a more strategic and practical part of the persuasion question: how can we become more effective in our persuasion efforts? What can we do or say that is more likely to influence others? In this section, we examine the traditional persuasion techniques of communication. Several broad types of persuasive communicative techniques have been isolated. These categories can be rather useful in that they give a sense of the factors that are capable of influencing others and what categories of persuasive forces there are.

Reciprocity and Social Proof

In one of the best-known examples of how reciprocity can be used in negotiation, Harold Kelley conducted a laboratory study in which he arranged for a group of students to be given either a small or a large can of Coca-Cola by an apparently disinterested individual. When the students were asked to rate this individual on a variety of scales, a significant positive difference was noted in the feelings held by those who had received the larger can of drink.

Social norms and conventions play a large part in how people communicate with each other. While the practice of negotiation does depend strongly on existing power structures built upon disparity in various resources, it is important to note that negotiation also takes place within a wider context, with many social pressures operating on both the individual negotiator and the negotiation process as a whole. These societal influences can facilitate fair and harmonious settlements in situations where economic forces alone may have led to cutthroat competition and strife. In this context, the notion of reciprocity - the giving and taking of positive (or negative) actions in mutual exchange - becomes an issue of great relevance. When one party makes a concession, the desire to reciprocate the generosity shown can be a powerful factor influencing the response of the other party. Many people, in describing a successful negotiation, will point out the importance of not seeking to over-exploit an opponent's goodwill.

Scarcity and Authority

The third process that underlies the social power of authority figures centers on the content of the information that these individuals possess. Authority figures utilize their sources of information in order to maintain their influence and control. Individuals who dominate decision-making in institutions utilize the beliefs of others and manipulate their knowledge.

Few of us like to pass judgment, and obeying authority makes it easier to avoid responsibility for our decisions. The other side of being an authority is that almost all of us are inclined to delegate decision-making to those whom we perceive as authorities in certain areas. In other words, many of us who are not authorities prefer to follow those who are. Furthermore, how other people arise their authority, whether it is through genuine or spurious means, is usually of less consequence than the fact that somebody has perceived authority.

The reason that many of us tend to like and, as a consequence, obey authority figures is that doing so frequently brings us significant well-being. For example, we do what our physicians tell us to stay healthy, we do what police officers tell us in order to steer clear of traffic tickets and the concomitant fines, we try to please our teachers to do better on exams, and we respond to our supervisors to avoid the anxieties of losing our jobs. Moreover, in hierarchically organized societies, individuals tend to maintain the status quo by deferring to authority figures whose decisions seem rational, based on normative guidelines and other accepted procedures or standards.

Another set of influence tactics involves scarcity principles and the use of authority. One particularly effective manner of increasing one's persuasiveness involves indicating or stating that one's proposal or conclusions represent a unique and rare opportunity, albeit in a subtle manner. The evidence of research has shown that the more rare a commodity appears to be, the greater the demand for it tends to be. In fact, we have noted earlier that simply knowing that information is being kept from an individual may make it seem more important, persuasive, or unique than its content might otherwise warrant.

CHAPTER 8

Applications of Persuasion in Marketing and Advert

Today, most advertising strategies, as suggested by Shimp, are designed to persuade the consumer to purchase a product or perform a specific behavior; and, in general, the strategies and theoretical concepts reviewed in this psychological field are used in advertising the situation. In a number of situations, advertising does persuade the recipient to perform the intended behavior, and this effect is maintained over time.

Persuasion is one of the areas of research that most interacts with the world of marketing and advertising. Every day, consumers are exposed to television commercials, sales strategies, publicity in the press, and other forms of persuasive communication with the objective of making them change their attitudes, buy a product, favor one brand in particular, or request a service or product. Therefore, on many occasions, advertising plays the advertiser's role as the communicator, who tries to convince the consumer to buy what they are being persuaded to purchase. Persuasion and advertising are inseparable in our society and are two of the most frequent topics studied by researchers.

Brand Loyalty and Consumer Behavior

A practical implementation of this irrational level of loyalty is that a well-respected or well-known brand is able to charge a higher price for its products. Thus, understanding how influence works in the field of business has tremendous implications. But when does brand loyalty become a problem? Brand loyalty becomes a problem when legality comes into play. It is funny how much a person is willing to do to protect a brand for which he or she is loyal, including breaking the law. Such people would go on online forums and defend the brand with half-truths in order to build its reputation as a company. Some would even go so far as to bring a lawsuit against someone who has publicly insulted or criticized their brand.

Brand loyalty is a behavior that demonstrates a psychological connection between a brand and a consumer. There are factors that influence brand loyalty, and one of them is brand trust. When a person trusts a brand, he or she is less willing to consider products from other brands, even if those products are of lower quality. Advertising and the media contribute to brand loyalty either by portraying the brand in the right way or by portraying competitors in a negative way. Thus, it can be said that brand loyalty is a funny thing: it forces people to behave irrationally as they are willing to buy an inferior product just because it's from a brand they trust. That is why people criticize the same brands to which they are willing to behave irrationally loyal.

Celebrity Endorsements

Recent research, however, suggests that although people might listen to the celebrity in advertising, these endorsements may not actually persuade people to buy the product. Overall, celebrity endorsements do not seem to be overly powerful techniques for actually persuading people to make purchasing decisions unless the celebrity is an expert in the product area. The whole of celebrity endorsements is actually based on mere-exposure theory, in that people are more likely to be favorable toward a product or idea that is familiar and well liked. The end result is that people will buy products from well-liked celebrities unless he/she is seen as an expert. The psychological mechanism based on persuasion research has to do with message repetition, much like the mere-exposure effect does. Therefore, celebrity endorsements are useful more for public attention-getting purposes than for persuading specific individuals.

Endorsements have been used to promote everything from soap to political candidates. They are prevalent in part because of a rather simple psychological notion: people are more likely to believe something if an accepted or reputable source, such as a celebrity or expert, says it, rather than if a seemingly biased source suggests the same thing. Behavior can be significantly influenced if the message is repeated enough times by a well-liked and respected individual.

CHAPTER 9

Persuasion in Politics and Public Policy

Belonging is the most important need because, as a social species, it's the one requirement for our survival. And the individual compulsion to belong has serious consequences for public policy. Research finds complete unanimity in the opinions of those who have a sense of belonging. Even when something is repeatedly opposed by a slight majority, a group of fewer than 30 people reports unanimous and strong opinions. The need to belong forces individuals to endorse policies that their colleagues hold dear, even if the policies are contrary to their own personal beliefs. Research also finds we are less open-minded when in groups. Individuals separated from the potential ridicule of a boisterous group dissent freely, and this freedom of thought and expression ensures that the best ideas are being discussed and pursued.

Psychologist Mark Leary once gave a group of students a rating scale and asked them to privately rate their worst fears. Then in a second part of the study, students were again asked to rate those same fears but this time with the knowledge that the ratings would soon be shared with a roomful of students and a panel of faculty members. Unsurprisingly, the fears on this second list were much smaller.

People had reduced the intensity of their fears because they feared losing face in front of their peers. It's understandable that fitting in leads us away from our normal behavior and toward what is acceptable. The need to belong can lead to remarkable behavior.

The most important kind of freedom is to be what you really are. You trade in your reality for a role. You trade in your sense for an act. You give up your ability to feel, and in exchange, put on a mask.

Political Campaigns and Propaganda

The stakes are very high in politics; psychological influence receives an enormous amount of strategic focus and financial resources from the candidates. Political experts often are very knowledgeable about the legal and ethical issues surrounding communication activities. But they deliberately employ several psychological tactics to separate you from your carefully guarded opinion. This is why I am a strong believer that education is a prerequisite prior to viewing propaganda, regardless of its form. By understanding what's behind the screen, you'll be much less susceptible to these everyday attempts to divert your life.

Political candidates and their staff are extremely concerned with the art of mastering influence. Years of research and study have revealed how to influence the thoughts and opinions of the undecided. Voters and potential donors are exposed to a barrage of persuasion tactics disguised as campaign advertising. They vary in sophistication and potency; because the candidates' presentation effort doesn't stop once a person has viewed a message only once, individuals may be exposed to the same message time and time again.

Behavioral Insights in Policy Making

1. Acknowledge unsustainable routines. Behavioral insights show that any particular behavior results from a mix of intentional

decisions and routine. Routinized and habitual actions are performed automatically, with a minimum of conscious deliberation. They are often the result of 'behavioral friction', such as emotional, social, or cognitive barriers to doing something otherwise easy, good, or right. The person faces 'self-control problems', prioritizing smaller short-term benefits and immediate pleasure over larger long-term benefits or expressing somebody else's preferences (e.g., a more present-focused or less responsible self). Because of these behavioral frictions, it is often challenging to make people stick to their resolutions. To implement decisions, structures providing sufficient patience, self-control, and willpower are needed. Agencies, therefore, must provide individuals with shortcuts that reinforce routine and structure and sustain motivation toward desired outcomes, enabling them to behave as if the future really matters.

2. Interventions must reflect a deep understanding of context and emotions. People make decisions based on the information they have, as well as on the way that information is presented to them. This means that when somebody is in a cognitive or emotional context where they know a lot, they are more able to rely on their own reasoning for making a decision. However, if someone is in an emotional or cognitive context where they do not know much or care much about the issue, they are more likely to rely on simple contextual features to guide their decisions. When making decisions, people will heavily weight anything that is particularly salient or easy to interpret. Different framing can therefore have dramatic effects on decision-making. This is why the initial presentation of intelligence to potential students or civil service careers at job fairs can have such an enormous impact by shaping and editing these information sets before the consumers apply, examine the criteria, engage in deliberation, and make a decision. Therefore, the context and framing of how and when information is experienced matter a lot to the nature

of the decisions that are made. A deep understanding of context and emotions is therefore needed in order to drive the decisions in a desired direction.

CHAPTER 10

Persuasion in Interpersonal Relationships

B ut despite our suspicions, to paraphrase in a slightly different way what Bennis, Gardner, Latham, and Watts say at the beginning of this chapter, there is always going to be persuasion in our lives, because as we have noted since the first edition, discreet interpersonal influence is an essential vehicle for making good things happen in the world. How is it a problem? It is a problem because the pervasiveness of social influence makes it a seductive weapon that "puts power in the hands of people who lack integrity." Seductive because according to some research, "Just as when we first fasten our seatbelt in a car, these initial small commitments to a certain course of action assure that we remain committed to continue that course of action to the end." They put power in the hands of people who have less integrity because even the most tender and self-aware of us aren't always men of principle in our dealings with others.

In politics, propagandists and demagogues try to make us think and act in certain ways. In the world of sales and advertising, pressure agents and schemers attempt to manipulate us into parting with our money or other assets. And in the field of social relations (especially romantic social relations), some people try to use persuasive strategies and tactics to win our cooperation and support. Used ethically, persuasiveness has the potential to be a positive, helpful force in this world - but as any of us who have ever been hoodwinked, bamboozled, and/or hornswoggled can testify, there are times when "winning friends and influencing people" seems like an odious part of the social and political upheaval that just keeps happening to us.

Conflict Resolution and Negotiation

Key principles during a negotiation include the desire for reciprocity, the need for consistency, the value of equity, the effects of self-perception, and the benefits of using reinforcement. By applying these concepts, negotiators save time, avoid conflict, and develop better working relationships. This article explores the principles of persuasion and demonstrates how they relate to dispute resolution, negotiation, and persuasion situations that arise through negotiation. We propose eight specific strategies of negotiation to accomplish two of the central goals of negotiation.

In negotiation, people constantly attempt to persuade others to do what they want them to do. Negotiators use choices and actions to express their preferences, influence the other side, and resolve specific conflicts. In making these choices, negotiators use persuasion principles to get the other side to accept an agreement, to give up something of value to the negotiator, or to modify a proposal to make it more acceptable to the other side. Other persuasion principles illustrate how negotiators attempt to influence a target of influence in a way that alters the nature of the relationship and the values that apply to a proposed negotiation.

Family Dynamics

Just as we adopt certain behaviors and reactions from our parents (possibly not because we want to, sometimes refuting identical behaviors but that we saw repeated) intentional coercion steps in to force some subduing. In order to capture the motivations that support those subduing dynamics, we are going to take into account external factors (as an intelligence measure for example) and get to the intimate sphere—internal factors—decisions typically characterized by an analysis of the relationship model: love, friendship, support, and communication adequacy. Intimacy is, therefore, a necessary ingredient for the birth of subduing and, in particular, for the birth of submission that is characterized as the active part of subduing.

We could not talk about the subject of influence without at least referring to one of its most significant spheres of operation: the influence and power systems of family relations. Family dynamics have been developed through time and countless studies and very often x-ray the mental processes of relationships that extend far beyond family, partners, and friendships. We can, therefore, see in the essence of many individual behaviors, reactions, and decisions strategic plans born in families, adulthood crises become typical behaviors revealed in family counseling, customer profiles that are repeatedly described as conditioned by familial directives and even market studies focusing only on families' or life partners' influence with regard to daily shopping. Family dynamics also stand out by frequently identifying the models of cooperation, confrontation, and negotiation alternate between the parts. Separations, inheritances, and compliment associated with the stages of life crises reaffirm this constant: inside families, life rarely just goes by.

CHAPTER 11

The Future of Persuasion Research

New constructs and refinements of existing variables generally add breadth and depth to the field. These developments reveal how influential others' behaviors are perceived, how that perception is affected by the characteristics of the observer, perceiver, or recipient, and how these characteristics play a role in mediating these effects. In the end, it is hoped that greater insight into these issues will allow researchers to explain why influence occurs, who is likely to be influenced, and under what conditions. The long-term goal of persuasion research should be to reveal the fundamental building blocks of the psychological architecture that makes social influence possible.

There is evidence that research in this area is becoming more multidisciplinary. Different traditions are more complementary than contradictory, and we are in an excellent position to uncover the full story of social influence in all its facets and dimensions. Social cognition is beginning to play a greater role in the field after being only slightly represented in the past, and a variety of new models and theories are being developed. Interest in chronic versus situational influence has burgeoned and is advancing through more sophisticated instruments and design as well as the continued development and integrative testing of existing theoretical models. The future also looks bright for the development of functional, structural, and dispositional models, as well as extensions of current models beyond their initial domains.

Neuroscience and Persuasion

The influence of a persuasive message depends on how it is presented. Current marketing claims often reflect the precise role of the brain in influencing preferences. The claims are often oversimplified or not adequately supported by experimental evidence, more specifically, by neuroimaging studies. The hype area has emerged as companies, often referred to as "neuromarketers," see market potential in understanding how the brain contributes to real-world marketing and advertising decisions. Even academic scientists, colleagues, and scientific institutions are beginning to capitalize on this "buzz," and there is increased interest to publish their findings in alternative, less traditional outlets. The goal of this chapter is to ensure that, regardless of whether one agrees or disagrees conceptually or strategically with the practice, individuals will be conscious of existing evidence and be better informed about how the brain is being incorporated into the science of marketing and persuasion.

The role of the brain in persuasion is an emerging interdisciplinary field. Persuasion lies at the intersection of psychological science, neuroscience, economics, and communication. The brain makes preferences that guide purchasing decisions and behavioral choices. These preferences have been traditionally assessed through indirect expressions such as self-reports of how much a person likes or wants a product. However, with the advent of functional neuroimaging techniques, the neural correlates of preferences and persuasive stimuli can be monitored as they unfold, thus advancing our understanding of the link between neural processing and preferences or choices.

Virtual Reality and Persuasion

In the effort to improve communication effectiveness, researchers have begun experimenting with virtual reality as a method of delivering information to an audience. Immersive VR provides a truly different form of presentation in which the audience can be placed at, and even within, the same context as the presented-media content, be it in ancient Greece or eighteenth-century Paris, an active war zone, or a computer-generated world of the future. Immersive VR has a great deal to offer, especially in creating an engaging audience experience, which is a critical factor in the attention-keeping aspect of communication. Virtual reality can provide an audience a direct, though artificial, representation of the original context in which a presentation of information was embedded by physically embedding the audience in a computer-generated synthetic environment, giving us the ability to create media presentations with texture, depth, and connection to both the story being told and the audience. That use of virtual reality is like watching a story embedded in its original environment through an open window with a significant amount of control over the story, including the capacity to look around and to bypass time and space in order to do so.